# Black Cat

Natalie Scott
Illustrated by Monique de Zoete

**CELEBRATION PRESS**
Pearson Learning Group

Black Bean is a cat.

He lives at the top of a high building. When he was a kitten he was carried up in a shoe box. He belongs to Emily Lopez.

Black Bean never goes out. Emily Lopez goes out, and sometimes Black Bean wonders why, although not for long. "I have no complaints," he purrs. "I'm snug and happy here."

Black Bean stretches on Emily Lopez's bed, curls up in her red velvet chair, and rolls on her carpet. He even twangs the strings of Emily Lopez's guitar. She doesn't mind. She loves him.

However, one night, on Emily Lopez's balcony—where the sky seems closer than the streets below—Black Bean feels a longing. It creeps up his spine. His back arches, his fur bristles. He feels a longing to see more of the world.

Down below, the city spreads like a carpet, rippling with the dots that are people, and the bigger dots that are cars and buses and trucks.

Black Bean begins to itch. Emily Lopez powders him regularly with "Flea Free," but it's not that sort of itch. It's an itch to be out in the world. Smells tickle and tease his whiskers.

"Black Bean," Emily Lopez calls, and she puts his saucer of milk alongside his bowl of sardines.

Monday: flounder

Tuesday: shrimp

Wednesday: mackerel

Thursday: cod

Friday: salmon

Saturday: tuna

Sunday: sardines. It must be Sunday.

The next morning Black Bean tries to forget the longing, but it's twice as strong as it was. Then it grows stronger . . . and Black Bean begins to feel sorry for himself.

"I'll grow thin and pale with this longing," he sighs. "I could die of it. I can't let that happen."

On Friday the door stands open, and Black Bean slips through. Heart thumping, he races down the hall . . . so many stairs! He leaps down three at a time—if he doesn't get on with it, he'll lose his nerve.

Down, down, down . . . then out into the world.

Tail high, he blinks and his blood stirs in him like a pudding. He sees strange and wonderful things: mailboxes, coffee shops, lamp posts, and dogs. This is the life: fountains and parks where the flowers grow in gardens, not in vases as he thought. There are streets, shops, traffic lights . . . and people. Hundreds of them. Maybe thousands!

Things move so fast, he's dizzy. When a bike almost knocks him over and the wheels of a bus squeal nearby, he dodges into a narrow side street. He huddles on a doorstep . . . scared.

A patched-up alley cat ambles Black Bean's way, and then looks him up and down. "What's the matter with you?" scratches out from its throat.

"It's . . . it's the traffic, the . . . the people, the noise and the—"

"You're scared," mutters the alley cat, and cleans a ragged ear. "If you'd seen the sights I've seen, you'd have plenty to be scared about." Its eyes gleam nastily. "I'm a real cat, not a house cat that sleeps on cushions and knows nothing of the world." It cleans the other ear. "What's your name?"

"Black Bean."

"Black Bean," it scoffs. "What a laugh! Jelly Bean's more like it, the way you're wobbling on a doorstep, shivering with fright."

And the alley cat humps its back, hisses, and goes about its business.

It's night again, and Black Bean wanders the streets. His tummy rumbles. He's hungry, and he can't stop thinking of his saucer of milk and the bowl of food Emily Lopez gives him—without fail.

He tries to cheer himself up. "This won't do. It won't get me anywhere." Suddenly his whiskers twitch.

"Do I smell fish?" He presses his nose to a shop window and begins to drool. Red fish, white fish, yellow fish, long and short, are laid on trays side by side, but out of reach!

A tabby cat with a sharp face bumps him. "Come with me," she winks, and streaks off, Black Bean close behind.

With a grumping, yowling, howling bunch of cats they wait at the back door of the fish shop. A boy comes out heaving a basket of fish heads. He dumps the load before slamming the door with a bang.

Black Bean scraps and snaps with the rest. He gulps the fish down. He's never eaten as fast as this in his life.

When the sharp-looking tabby follows him into the night, Black Bean no longer feels dreamy or satisfied. He feels sick. Lamp posts wobble as he sways from side to side. What's more, the pavements are hard and his paws hurt. "Ooooh," he groans.

"What's up? You look strange," the tabby says. "Green."

"What do you mean? I'm Black Bean."

She smirks. "Green Bean's a better name for you." Then she shrugs, and goes about her business.

A storm is brewing. Thunder rolls, and heavy clouds lump in the sky. Black Bean has never been out in a storm. People run for shelter, and the cats of the city scoot for cover.

"Where should I go, where should I go?" Black Bean whimpers, and his tail flicks as the rain comes down. Then something leaps between his paws. In alarm he looks down to see a smoky-blue kitten curled against him. Close. "What do you want?"

"To stay with you." Its voice is thin and afraid. "To be safe."

Now the rain is as sharp as needles. What should they do? Black Bean knows he must lead off and find somewhere dry, or they'll end up sopping wet. The storm lashes the city.

At last the rat-a-tat becomes a pit-a-pat.

When the rain stops, the kitten is playful. Rolling about, it snaps at the air. "What's your name?" it asks in a squeaky voice.

"Black Bean."

"No, you must be Broad Bean," it meows. "Because you've been broad and warm for me." Then chasing its tail and failing to catch it, it scampers away, off on its own business.

Black Bean has been roaming about for days and can't decide if he likes it or not. This wide world is exciting, yet it's lonely.

Down at the city markets he's seen a beautiful cat. She's tall and her sleek fur is the color of toffee. One day, her golden eyes stare straight at Black Bean, but the next moment she looks straight through him, as if he's invisible, not there.

Black Bean wants to be noticed. So does a big, gray, grumpy rock of a cat who hisses and spits when he catches sight of him. Black Bean has enough sense to watch out, just in case.

The next morning Black Bean purrs as the toffee-colored cat slinks toward him . . . Zing! Out of nowhere like a bolt of lightning, the gray, grumpy cat claws through the air.

Black Bean shoves and tugs, but he doesn't put up much of a fight. His tail shoots up, he braces to spring . . . too late. Claws rip his fur. This gray, grumpy cat has been fighting all of its life.

Bruised, scruffy, and sad, Black Bean watches as the beautiful lady sticks her nose in the air and goes about her business.

Black Bean aches all over until he feels a hand pat him, sliding gently from his head to his tail.

"Poor old cat," a voice croons. "That gray, grumpy cat thinks you're a scaredy."

Scaredy! Scaredy! He's no scaredy cat. He's Black Bean, and that's who he'll always be.

Black Bean wanders on, exploring the world. The Sun rises and sets, the Moon and stars shine then fade. Time passes. Then out of the blue, he feels a longing, a longing for home.

Is his home still there? Where is it? Buildings sprout on every side like concrete beanstalks. How will he find his—

Where is Emily Lopez?

He climbs hundreds of stairs, but they're all the wrong stairs—until one morning, sad and miserable, he huddles down at the door of yet another high building, and begins to cry.

The longing to be home with Emily Lopez is now stronger than the longing to see more of the world. He hurts all over, and his tears catch on his whiskers.

"Crying won't help," he tells himself. Instead he closes his eyes and begins to dream. He dreams of Emily Lopez. In the dream he's curled up on her favorite red chair. He even hears the twang of Emily Lopez's guitar. This is so good; he wants to keep his eyes closed forever.

Slowly he opens one eye, then the other. This can't be true! There sits Emily Lopez playing the guitar. Now she's fondling his ears, gathering him up in her arms.

"Where's my Black Bean?" she murmurs. "It seems I've lost him forever. When I saw you by the door, so thin and straggly, I thought with a shock: here's a little String Bean. My beautiful Black Bean has gone off to see the world, and—"

Black Bean leaps out of her arms and runs in circles like a wild thing. "I AM YOUR BLACK BEAN, I AM!"

"Are you?" Emily Lopez frowns and squints hard.

"Yes, yes, YES! I'm no Jelly Bean, no Green Bean, no Broad Bean. I'm not a scaredy cat or a straggly String Bean. I am BLACK BEAN!"

Emily Lopez stares. She stares hard, and her eyes begin to shine. "So you are." Lovingly she strokes him, then twirls his tail through her fingers before she goes off to fetch his saucer of milk and his bowl of sardines.

Sardines?

Sardines! It must be Sunday!